T0050907

Pebble Plus

Hands-On Science Fun

How to Make BUBBLES

Revised Edition

by Erika L. Shores

Consultant: Ronald Browne, PhD
Department of Elementary & Early Childhood Education
Minnesota State University, Mankato

4D

Download the Capstone 4D app for additional content.

See page 2 for directions.

CAPSTONE PRESS
a capstone imprint

Download the Capstone 4D app!

- Ask an adult to search in the Apple App Store or Google Play for "Capstone 4D".
- Click Install (Android) or Get, then Install (Apple).
- Open the app.
- Scan any of the following spreads with this icon:

When you scan a spread, you'll find fun extra stuff to go with this book!
You can also find these things on the web at www.capstone4D.com
using the password: **bubbles.09472**

Pebble Plus is published by Capstone Press,
1710 Roe Crest Drive, North Mankato, Minnesota 56003
www.mycapstone.com

Copyright © 2018 by Capstone Press, a Capstone imprint.
All rights reserved. No part of this publication may be reproduced in whole or in part, or stored in a retrieval system, or transmitted in any form or by any means, electronic, mechanical, photocopying, recording, or otherwise, without written permission of the publisher.

Library of Congress Cataloging-in-Publication Data
is available on the Library of Congress website.

ISBN 978-1-5435-0947-2 (library binding)
ISBN 978-1-5435-0953-3 (paperback)
ISBN 978-1-5435-0959-5 (ebook pdf)

Editorial Credits
Marissa Kirkman, editor; Sarah Bennett, designer; Tracy Cummins, media researcher; Tori Abraham, production specialist

Photo Credits
Capstone Studio: Karon Dubke, Cover, 3, 4, 5, 7, 9, 11, 13, 15, 17, 19, 21; Shutterstock: Alena Ohneva, Design Element (Bubbles)

Note to Parents and Teachers

The Hands-On Science Fun set supports national science standards related to physical science. This book describes and illustrates how to make soap bubbles. The images support early readers in understanding the text. The repetition of words and phrases helps early readers learn new words. This book also introduces early readers to subject-specific vocabulary words, which are defined in the Glossary section. Early readers may need assistance to read some words and to use the Table of Contents, Glossary, Read More, Internet Sites, Critical Thinking Questions, and Index sections of the book.

Printed in the United States 4459

Table of Contents

Getting Started 4

Making Bubbles 6

How Does It Work?. 18

Glossary 22

Read More. 23

Internet Sites 23

Critical Thinking Questions 24

Index 24

Safety Note:
Please ask an adult for help when making bubbles.

Getting Started

Bubbles float in the sink. Bubbles pop in a glass of soda. Mix together simple ingredients and make your own super bubbles.

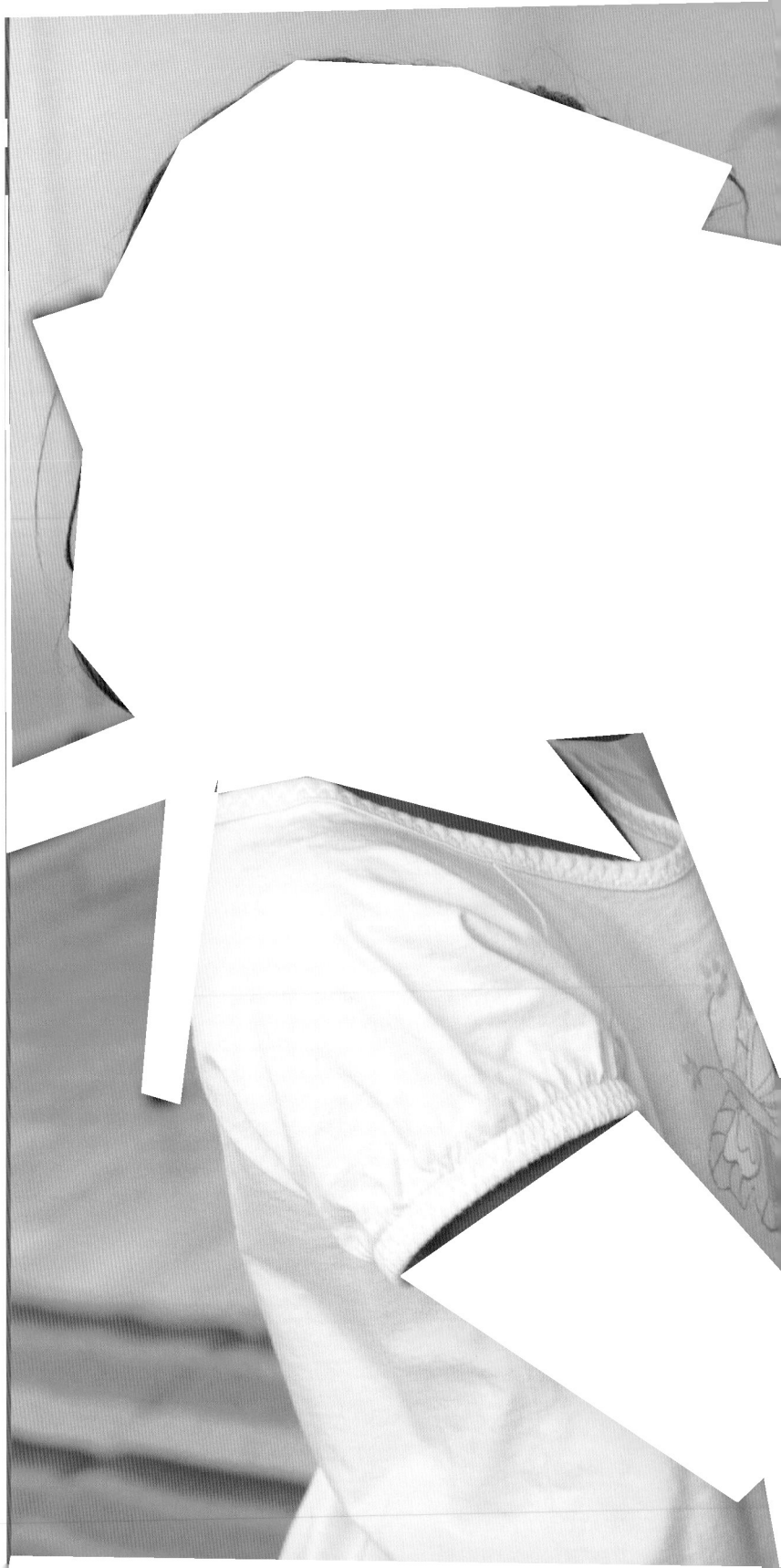

Here's what you need:

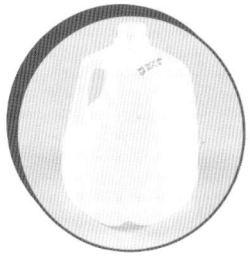

1 gallon (4 L)
warm water

1 cup (240 mL)
dish soap

1 tablespoon (15 mL)
glycerin (sold at drugstores)

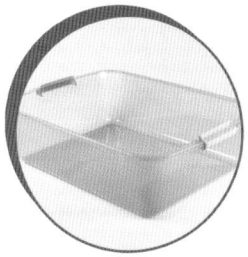

large plastic tub

spoon

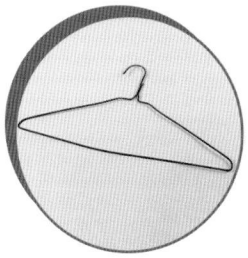

wire coat hanger

drinking straw, potato masher,
spatula, or other utensils
with holes

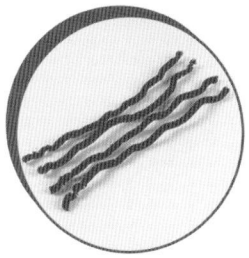

pipe cleaners

Making Bubbles

Pour 1 gallon of warm water into a large plastic tub.

Add 1 cup of dish soap.

Next, add 1 tablespoon of glycerin.

Slowly stir the mixture.

Try not to make suds.

Let the bubble mixture sit
for two or three days.

Make your own bubble wand
by shaping a wire hanger
into a circle.

Wrap pipe cleaners
around the hanger.

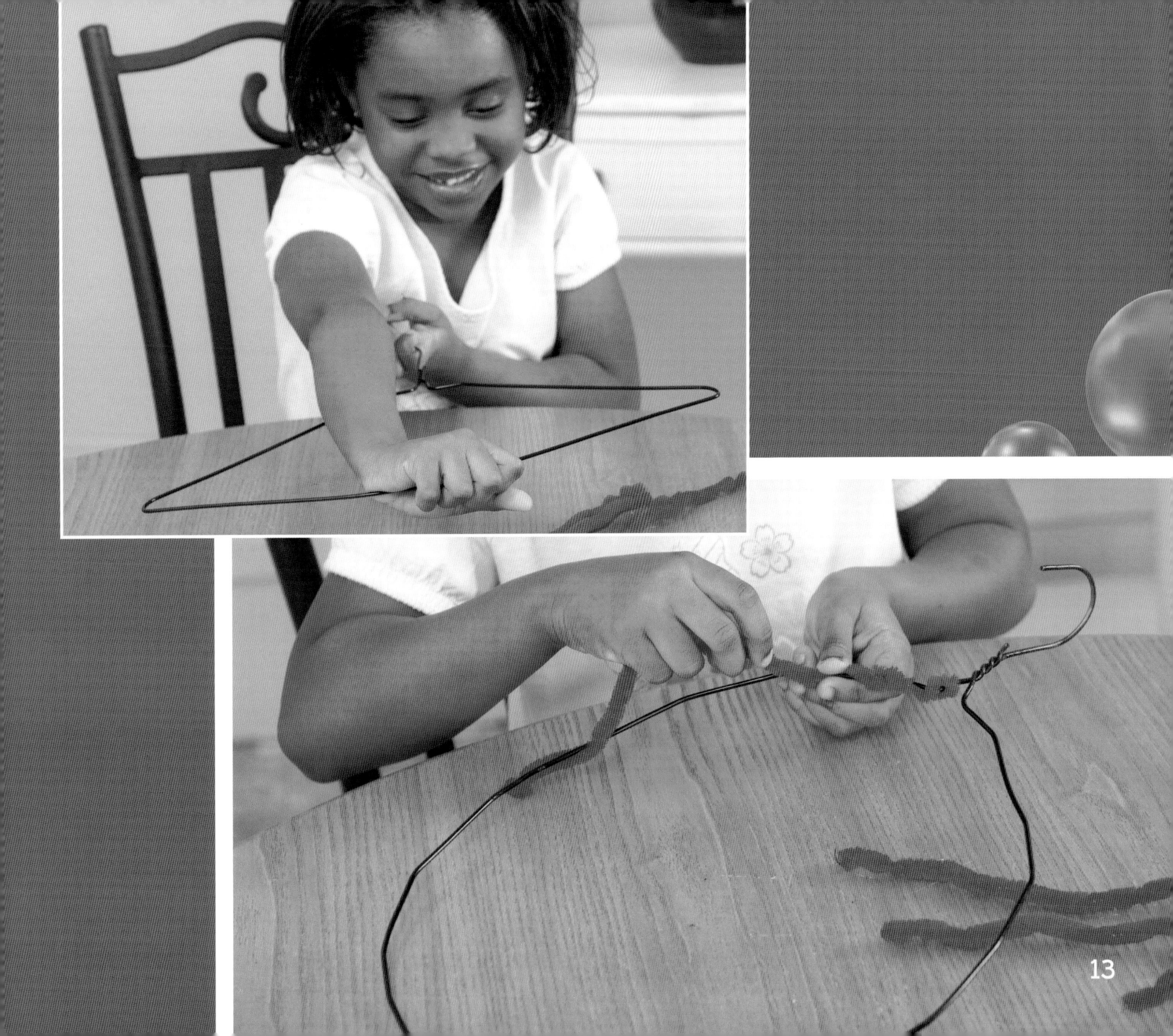

Ask an adult to carry
the tub outside.

Blow lots of bubbles with a straw.
Dip a potato masher into the tub.
Blow through the holes.

Put the hanger into the mixture.

Pull it out slowly. Gently move it through the air.

You may have to try several times before you make a giant bubble.

How Does It Work?

Blowing air can make a thin film of soap stretch. When stretched too far, the film snaps closed. Air trapped inside makes a round bubble.

Bubbles burst when they dry out.
The soapy film gets too thin
and the air inside escapes.
A bubble also breaks when
it touches something dry.

POP!

Glossary

burst—to break apart suddenly

escape—to get away from

film—a very thin layer of something

glycerin—a syrupy liquid used in soaps, perfumes, and other products

ingredient—an item used to make something else

mixture—something made up of different things mixed together

Read More

Challoner, Jack. *Maker Lab: 28 Super Cool Projects: Build, Invent, Create, Discover.* New York: DK Publishing, 2016.

Citro, Asia. *The Curious Kid's Science Book: 100+ Creative Hands-On Activities for Ages 4–8.* Woodinville, Wash.: Innovative Press, 2015.

Heinecke, Liz Lee. *Outdoor Science Lab for Kids: 52 Family-Friendly Experiments for the Yard, Garden, Playground, and Park.* Beverly, Mass.: Quarry Books, 2016.

Internet Sites

Use FactHound to find Internet sites related to this book.

Visit *www.facthound.com*

Just type **9781543509472** and go.

Critical Thinking Questions

1. What happens when a thin film of soap is stretched too far?
2. What can cause bubbles to break?
3. What other items do you think you could use to make bubbles with your bubble mixture?

Index

air, 16, 18, 20
bubble wands, 12
bursting, 20
dish soap, 8
film, 18, 20
glycerin, 8
hangers, 12, 16
pipe cleaners, 12
potato mashers, 14
straws, 14
stretching, 18
water, 6